The Ultimate Guide to Infant's Early Life

I0558608

"Embracing the journey of nurturing growth, development, and happiness from birth to two!" Essential Tips, Game-Changing Milestones, and Expert Insights to Boost Your Child's Development

Adegboye S. Aduragbemi

INTRODUCTION

The journey to parenting is one of the great paths of motherhood that every upcoming, new, and matured couples are expected to understand before embarking on it.

From the minute your kid enters the world, they begin a fascinating journey of growth, discovery, and development. As a parent, it is natural to have questions and concerns about your baby's progress and well-being, especially during the vital early years of their life.

In this book, we are happy to give a complete guide to understanding and supporting your baby's development from birth to two years of age. From their very first milestones to the thrilling successes of toddlerhood, each chapter is dedicated to addressing typical questions and concerns that parents may have regarding their child's growth and development.

This book is filled with a plethora of questions and answers, knowledge, advice, and tools to support you as a parent and help you deal with the pleasures and difficulties of raising a child at each developmental stage. We are here to support you on your parenting journey with expert insights, evidence-based guidance, and valuable methods, regardless of your concerns about your child's physical milestones, cognitive ability, or emotional well-being.

Remind yourself that you are not alone as you set out on this fantastic journey that is motherhood. Let's treasure each milestone, appreciate the wonder of infancy, and embrace the journey of raising your children as they develop and flourish.

Chapter One

Physical development stages of infants

When will my child begin to raise their head during tummy time?

During tummy time, which occurs between two and four months of age, most newborns start to raise their heads and chests off the ground. By putting your infant on their stomach for brief periods, multiple times a day, under supervision, you can promote this growth.

When do babies usually begin to sit on their own?

Between the ages of six and eight months, babies usually start to sit on their own. They could fall or need assistance at first, but with time and effort, they'll gain the strength and balance necessary to sit on their own.

When can I expect my infant to begin rolling over?

Between six and ten months of age, babies usually begin to crawl; however, some may skip crawling entirely and start pulling themselves up and cruising along furniture instead.

What are the usual walking and standing milestones?

Between the ages of 8 and 12 months, babies typically pull themselves up to stand, and between the ages of 9 and 15 months, many take their first independent steps. Infants vary significantly in their ability to walk; some may not start to walk until they are closer to 18 months of age or even later.

How can I help my infant develop physically in these formative years?

By giving your infant lots of chances for movement and exploration in a secure setting, you can aid in their physical development. Provide toys that encourage reaching and gripping, boost tummy time, and provide opportunities for crawling, cruising, and eventually walking.

Some babies seem to pick up physical abilities more slowly than my infant. Do I need to worry?

As each baby develops at their own rate, there is no set standard for what constitutes normal development. While comparing your baby's development to others is normal, try to concentrate on their unique qualities and developmental milestones. But don't be afraid to talk to your pediatrician about any worries you may have regarding your baby's physical development.

How and when should I introduce solid foods to my baby?

While some babies may be ready to start solids a little earlier or later, most newborns are ready to start solids at about six months of age. Start with simple, iron-rich purees like rice cereal, pureed fruits, or pureed vegetables. As your baby expresses interest and is ready, gradually introduce more textures and flavors.

How can I get my child to play physically and become more active?

Provide lots of chances for outdoor and indoor active play. Go for walks, visit playgrounds, and give items (such as balls, ride-on toys, and climbing structures) that help develop gross motor skills. Set a good example for your child by exercising yourself and recognizing their accomplishments.

What safety precautions should I take into account as my kid grows more mobile?

As your child grows more mobile, make sure your house is babyproofed by adding safety gates at the stairs, covering electrical outlets, and securing furniture. Keep small items and potential choking hazards out of your baby's reach and keep a watchful eye on them, especially when they are near stairs, water, and pets.

When is the right time to move my child from a crib to a toddler bed?

Depending on their preparedness and safety concerns, most children adjust from a crib to an infant bed between the ages of 18 months and three years old. To guarantee a seamless transition, watch for indications that your toddler is attempting to crawl out of the crib or showing interest in a big kid's bed.

How can I support my infant's development of fine motor skills?

Toys and activities that involve gripping, reaching, and manipulating objects, like rattles, stacking toys, and shape sorters, can help foster the development of fine motor skills. During mealtimes, give your infant lots of opportunities to practice using utensils and picking up little objects with their fingers.

When do babies usually begin to become coordinated with their hands and eyes?

Hand-eye coordination in babies starts to develop at birth, but by the time they are 4 or 6 months old, they may have made tremendous progress. Playing with soft toys or reaching for a dangling toy during tummy time are two activities that might help your baby develop hand-eye coordination because they require reaching for and grabbing objects.

My infant doesn't seem eager to try new foods and textures. How can I get them to sample different foods and textures?

Start with small portions and offer a range of flavors and textures when introducing new foods and textures. Let your baby use their hands and fingers to investigate meals; if they refuse at first, have patience with them. Reward your child with praise and encouragement when they try new meals; do not force or coerce them into eating.

If my child is not reaching physical developmental milestones, when should I get worried?

Even though each baby develops at a different rate, it's essential to keep an eye on your child's development and talk to your pediatrician about any worries. If your child routinely misses developmental milestones, exhibits severe delays or regression, or if you see any other indications of possible developmental problems, get them evaluated.

My toddler moves around a lot and is really active. How can I make sure kids exercise enough every day?

Throughout the day, give them chances to play and move actively both indoors and outside. Go for walks, visit playgrounds or parks, and promote physical activities like dancing, jumping, and jogging. Offer toys and activities that encourage physical activity and the development of gross motor skills in addition to limiting screen time.

What are some telltale signals that my child is getting close to walking instead of just crawling?

Your baby may be getting ready to move from crawling to walking when they can stand up on their own, cruise around furniture, and take a few steps while hanging onto assistance. Sure babies could express curiosity about standing up on their own and try walking without assistance.

How can I promote my baby's physical development by helping them build strong core muscles?

Encourage exercises that strengthen the core muscles, such as reaching, stretching, and balancing exercises, as well as belly time and supported sitting. Give your infant toys and play equipment, such as activity gyms, bouncers, and play mats, that will help them use their core muscles.

If my kid prefers to use one hand over the other, should I be concerned?

As early as six to twelve months of age, babies frequently exhibit handedness, the desire to use one hand over the other. Regularly not a cause for alarm. It is a typical stage of development. Talk to your pediatrician, though, if your child routinely refuses to use one hand or if you observe severe dominance.

When my kid is handled or has their diaper changed, they have a propensity to straighten their legs or arch their back. Is this typical?

Some babies use leg stiffness or back arching as a means of expressing discomfort or expressing their independence. To get further evaluated, speak with your pediatrician if you observe that these behaviors continue or are accompanied by other worrisome signs like irritability or feeding issues.

How can I safely encourage my child to experiment with climbing and balancing?

Give your child access to secure climbing areas and chances for them to practice climbing, such as playground climbing equipment that is appropriate for their age or climbing stairs under supervision. When your toddler is climbing, always keep a watchful eye on them and make sure there are no potential risks in the area.

Physical mobility and exploration phases of an infant's development

What can I do to encourage my baby to roll over, and when can I anticipate them to start doing so?

The majority of babies begin rolling over from their stomach to their back at 24 months and vice versa at 46 months. To help them roll, put engaging objects just out of reach and give them lots of supervised tummy time to help them attain this milestone.

When do babies usually start sitting up on their own, and how can I help them develop this skill?

Between the ages of 4 and 7 months, babies typically begin sitting up on their own. Using a Boppy cushion to support them during playing or propping them up with pillows will help you support this ability. Till they have gotten the hang of sitting, try not to leave them alone.

What kinds of crawling styles might my baby utilize, and when will they start?

Between six and ten months old, babies usually begin to crawl; however, some may skip crawling entirely and start pulling themselves up and cruising instead. There are several different ways to crawl: army crawling, bottom shuffling, and regular hands-and-knees crawling.

What can I do to give my crawling infant a secure environment?

Put safety gates at the top and bottom of staircases, cover electrical outlets, and secure furniture to help babyproof your house. When your baby is exploring, keep small items, choking hazards, and toxic chemicals out of their reach and keep a tight eye on them.

How can I assist my baby in learning how to pull themselves up to stand, and when should I anticipate them to start doing so?

Between the ages of six and twelve months, infants may begin to pull themselves to stand. Please encourage them to use this ability by setting up low tables or sturdy furnishings that they can grip onto to get up. To avoid tipping, make sure the furniture is secure and anchored.

When do newborns usually start cruising and walking while clinging to furniture, and how can I help them through this developmental stage?

Between the ages of 8 and 12 months, babies typically start to cruise. Create a secure space with lots of solid furnishings so they have something to grab onto to encourage them to cruise. Encourage and assist them as they make their way through the environment.

How soon can I expect my kid to walk, and when will they take their first steps?

While some newborns may begin earlier or later, most babies take their first unassisted steps between the ages of nine and twelve months. Give them opportunities to practice standing and walking while holding your hands or using push toys to help them develop their walking skills.

How can I promote sensory exploration, and what part does it play in physical development?

Feeling various textures is one way that babies can grow their well and gross motor skills through bodily exploration. Kindly give them a range of toys to grip, handle, and investigate that have varying textures, shapes, and sizes to promote sensory exploration.

How might playtime and movement activities help my baby's physical development?

Play with stacking toys, encourage crawling through tunnels or obstacle courses, or roll a soft ball back and forth as interactive play activities that enhance physical development.

What physical development milestones should I watch out for, and when should I be concerned?

Although each baby develops at their rate, you should see your pediatrician if you observe any notable delays or physical anomalies in your child, such as chronic favoring of one side of the body, trouble bearing weight on the legs, or asymmetrical movements.

What are some telltale signals that my child is prepared to walk on their own?

When your baby starts to stand up on their own, cruises confidently along furniture takes tiny steps while clinging to you, and expresses curiosity in walking alone, those are indications that they are ready to walk independently.

Should I help my infant learn to walk using a walker or other comparable equipment?

Walker use is generally discouraged by pediatricians since it might be dangerous and stunt motor development. Instead, assist your infant in learning to walk by giving them encouragement and the opportunity to practice in a secure setting.

How can I help my kid develop coordination and balance?

Ensure you encourage your child to play on uneven surfaces, like grass or sand, and give them toys that need two hands to reach, grab, and manipulate in order to improve balance and coordination.

Rather than crawling traditionally, my baby would rather crawl on their tummy. Is this typical?

Yes, a lot of babies take up their crawling gait, which may include bottom shuffling, army crawling, or belly crawling. Usually, there's no reason to worry about their favorite crawling manner as long as they're investigating and getting around securely.

How can I foster my infant's natural curiosity and exploration of their environment?

By furnishing a stimulating space with age-appropriate toys, reading material, and sensory elements, you can foster curiosity and discovery. Let your infant investigate various materials, noises, and textures while keeping an eye on them.

My infant appears reluctant to explore unfamiliar places. What can I do to make them more at ease?

Introduce new situations and experiences to your infant gradually to help them feel more at ease. Start in familiar surroundings and introduce new people, locations, and activities gradually, allowing them to adjust at their rate.

When can I anticipate my child to begin using stairs, and what steps can I take to make sure they stay safe?

Between the ages of 12 and 18 months, babies may begin to climb stairs. To mitigate the risk of falls, implement safety gates at both the upper and lower ends of staircases. Also, keep a constant eye on your infant whenever they are near stairs until they have mastered the art of climbing securely.

Is it typical for my infant to favor one hand over the other when using it?

Indeed, it's common for infants to exhibit hand dominance or a preference for one hand over the other, which usually appears at about 18 months of age. When engaging in activities that promote bilateral coordination and motor development, encourage the use of both hands.

If my child is not reaching physical milestones on schedule, should I be worried?

Even though each baby develops at their rate, if your infant is severely behind schedule on milestones or if you have concerns about their physical development, speak with your pediatrician.

What part does my baby's physical development play while we play outside?

Your baby can explore and participate in physical activities like crawling, walking, climbing, and running when they play outside. These activities are vital for the development of strength, coordination, and gross motor skills.

Growth monitoring and issues related to an infant's development

How can I monitor the development and growth of my infant?

By consistently documenting your baby's weight, length, and head circumference measurements on growth charts that healthcare practitioners offer, you can keep an eye on their development. To evaluate general development, keep an eye out for developmental milestones like rolling over, sitting up, crawling, and walking.

What developmental milestones should I anticipate my infant hitting in the first year of life?

Babies usually triple their birth weight by the end of the first year, having doubled it by about six months. They also get longer; in the first year, their length increases by an average of roughly 10 inches.

How often should my child's growth checkups be scheduled?

In the first year, well-baby checkups are usually scheduled every 12 months, but in the second year, the frequency of visits decreases. During these visits, medical professionals can keep an eye on the general health and growth of your child.

What are some indicators that the growth of my child should worry me?

Consistently falling below or above growth percentiles on growth charts, failing to gain weight or length at a typical rate, or a notable departure from anticipated developmental milestones are all indicators that something is wrong with your child's growth.

If I am worried about my baby's development or growth, what should I do?

Talk to your pediatrician if you have any worries regarding the growth or development of your child. They can perform developmental screenings, evaluate your baby's progress using standardized growth charts, and handle any underlying problems or concerns.

What elements can impact the development and growth of my baby?

A number of factors, such as prenatal and postnatal care, diet, genetics, general health, and environmental factors, can influence a baby's growth and development. The key to encouraging your baby's best development is figuring out what might be affecting their growth and taking appropriate action.

How can I help my baby grow and develop healthily?

Make sure your baby eats a healthy diet by nursing, using formula, or a mix of the two; introduce solid foods according to your pediatrician's recommendations; create a secure and engaging space for learning and exploration; and schedule routine well-baby exams and developmental screenings.

What are some warning signs of growth issues or developmental delays?

Significant delays in meeting developmental milestones, ongoing inability to gain weight or grow, aberrant head growth, peculiar physical characteristics, or other indicators of underlying health problems are all potential red flags for developmental delays or growth disorders.

What part does diet play in the development and growth of my baby?

In order to promote a baby's healthy growth and development, nutrition is essential. During the first year of life, breast milk or formula offers vital nutrients for growth; after six months, providing a variety of nutrient-dense solid foods helps meet your baby's growing nutritional needs.

How can I help my baby develop physically in a healthy way?

Your baby's neck, back, and arm muscles will strengthen with plenty of supervised tummy time. Give them safe opportunities to explore and move, such as playing with toys on the floor that are appropriate for their age and encouraging them to reach, grab, and crawl.

What are some indicators of skill loss or developmental regression?

Loss of previously learned skills, such as making eye contact, babbling, or meeting developmental milestones, can be a sign of developmental regression or loss of skills. Discuss any regression or worries you have with your pediatrician as soon as possible.

If my baby's weight or height falls into a lower percentile, should I be concerned?

Growth charts with percentiles are simply one tool for monitoring development and growth. If your kid is otherwise healthy, active, and reaching developmental milestones, then being in the lower percentile does not always mean that there is an issue. But if you're worried, speak with your pediatrician.

What part does genetics play in the growth and development of my child?

The way your baby grows, as well as its height, weight, and general physical attributes, can be influenced by genetics. However, your baby's growth and development are also greatly influenced by environmental factors, including nutrition, health, and caregiving.

When is the right time for my baby to switch from formula or breast milk to cow's milk?

Around 12 months of age, most babies can begin consuming cow's milk as their primary source of nutrition; however, for advice specific to your baby's requirements and development, speak with your pediatrician.

Chapter Two

Stages of cognitive development in newborns

When do infants begin to identify familiar things and faces?

During the first few months of life, babies usually start to remember faces and familiar objects, but with time, their recognition skills improve. Babies may discriminate between known faces by the time they are 3 to 6 months old, and they may express a preference for their primary caretakers or favorite toys.

When do infants start to grasp the concept of object permanence?

Around six or eight months of age is when object permanence, or the knowledge that items exist even when they are hidden from view, usually starts to take shape. Babies can show that they grasp this concept by looking for concealed objects or expressing surprise when things are out of sight.

How can I use play to support my baby's cognitive development?

Aside from interactive games and brightly illustrated books, you may stimulate your baby's cognitive development by letting them play with age-appropriate toys that promote problem-solving and discovery, like stacking blocks or shape sorters.

When do infants begin to mimic noises and movements?

Infants mimic noises and movements from an early age, frequently starting as early as a few weeks. Babies may begin mimicking basic movements, sounds, and activities they hear in their surroundings by the time they are nine or twelve months old.

When do babies usually start to comprehend basic instructions?

Around nine or twelve months of age is when babies usually start to understand simple orders like "wave bye-bye" or "give me the ball." Provide clear instructions that are supported by gestures or other actions to aid with comprehension.

When do infants begin to express curiosity about cause-and-effect dynamics?

From a very young age, babies have an interest in cause-and-effect interactions, yet, with time, this understanding develops into something more complex. Babies may start to enjoy simple cause-and-effect toys, like ones that light up or make noise when engaged, by the time they are six to nine months old.

What are some telltale signals that my child is becoming adept at solving problems?

When your baby tries different approaches to accomplish a task, like reaching for a toy that is out of reach or figuring out how to open a container to get its contents, it is a sign that they are beginning to solve difficulties. Babies may also demonstrate perseverance when attempting to complete easy tasks or puzzles.

How can I ensure my toddlers mentally develop as they become older?

By giving your toddler the chance to play freely, having discussions and telling stories, and introducing puzzles, games, and other activities that foster creativity and problem-solving at an appropriate age, you may help your child's cognitive development.

When do infants usually begin to demonstrate an interest in reading and books?

Even as early as a few months old, babies can already be displaying signs of interest in books and reading. Encourage this interest by reading to your infant on a regular basis and utilizing interactive, exciting books with straightforward language and vibrant illustrations.

How can I support my toddler's recall and memory development?

Repetitive activities and routines, which include reciting nursery rhymes or singing well-known songs, can aid your toddler's memory and recall development. You can also encourage them to recall incidents or events from their daily lives.

When do infants begin to comprehend concepts of time, such as day and night?

Babies learn about time through recurring experiences and everyday routines. By the time they are 6 to 12 months old, babies may begin to identify day and night patterns, such as waking and sleeping cycles, and they may also express preferences for particular activities at particular times of the day.

When do babies start showing signs of interest and investigating their environment?

Babies show signs of inquiry and interest from a very young age, often even from birth. But as they become older, their interest turns into something more deliberate and focused. Babies may actively seek out new experiences and have an interest in exploring their surroundings by the time they are nine or twelve months old.

When do infants learn to respond to and recognize their names?

Between the ages of six and twelve months, babies usually start to know and react to their names. When their name is uttered, they might first react somewhat or tilt their head in that direction, but with time, this response becomes more reliable.

How can I help my infant develop cognitively through regular interactions?

Talking, singing, and playing with your infant are examples of responsive and stimulating activities that you may do to encourage cognitive development through regular contact. By giving them toys, items, and experiences that are age-appropriate and pique their curiosity, you may promote their exploration and discovery.

When do infants begin to perceive depth and have an awareness of their surroundings?

From birth, babies start to perceive depth and have a feeling of spatial awareness, although this understanding develops with time. By the time they are 6 to 12 months old, newborns may begin to demonstrate an awareness of object distance and make more accurate movements to reach for objects at different distances.

What part does imitation play in infant and toddler cognitive development?

Because it enables infants to learn by seeing and copying the activities and behaviors of others, imitation is essential for cognitive development. Babies learn social and communication skills as well as the concepts of cause and consequence by mimicking noises and actions.

How can I use sensory experiences to help my baby's cognitive development?

Via giving your infant opportunities for sensory exploration and stimulation, such as via touching, tasting, smelling, seeing, and hearing a range of textures, objects, and environments, you can enhance their cognitive development through sensory experiences.

When do infants learn to recognize and employ gestures like waving and pointing?

Ranging from the age of nine and twelve months, babies usually start to comprehend and utilize gestures like pointing and waving. Babies use these gestures as early forms of communication to convey their needs, wants, and interests.

What part does infants' playtime with friends have in their cognitive development?

Toddlers can acquire and practice social skills, problem-solving, and perspective-taking during playtime with their friends. Toddlers develop their social and cognitive skills through interactive play, which teaches them to share, take turns, and collaborate.

What symptoms to watch out for and when should I be concerned about my baby's cognitive development?

Even though each baby develops at a different rate, it's essential to keep an eye on their growth and see a pediatrician if you have any worries about their cognitive development. Significant delays or regressions in milestones, a lack of interest in their environment, or ongoing challenges with communication and problem-solving are indications that may call for more assessment.

Sensory and cognitive development phases of infants

Throughout the first year of life, how do infants develop their senses?

Infants quickly develop their senses during the first year of life through interaction and exploration of their surroundings. Their heightened sensitivity to sights, sounds, tastes, smells, and textures aids in their understanding of their surroundings.

What are some early indicators that my infant is starting to notice their environment?

Early indicators of enhanced awareness include turning toward familiar voices, grabbing and reaching for objects, tracking moving objects with their eyes, and displaying interest in bright or contrasted patterns.

When do newborns usually begin to express preferences for particular toys or pastimes?

As early as 36 months of age, babies may begin to exhibit preferences for particular toys or activities. Toys with vibrant colors, sounds, or a variety of textures to explore may pique their interest.

In what ways does infants' sensory exploration aid in their cognitive development?

Babies learn about cause and effect, object permanence, and spatial relationships through sensory exploration, which is a crucial input for cognitive development. It also promotes curiosity, problem-solving abilities, and brain development.

What part does playtime play in the cognitive and sensory development of infants?

Infants can develop cognitive abilities like spatial awareness, problem-solving, and creative thinking during playtime by participating in sensory-rich activities. A variety of play styles, including pretend play, sensory play, and exploratory play, promote different facets of development.

How can I provide my infant with a sensory-rich environment to aid in their development?

Give your baby access to a range of materials and toys that have various textures, shapes, and sounds so they can explore them. Provide opportunities for tactile play, like sand, water, and soft materials. To encourage cognitive development and awaken your baby's senses, engage them in sensory play activities.

What regular interactions can I do to support my baby's cognitive development?

Play easy games like hide-and-seek, pat-a-cake, and peekaboo to help develop cognitive abilities like memory, problem-solving, and object permanence. Encourage experimentation and discovery while offering lots of chances for practical learning.

When do babies usually begin to show signs of being able to solve problems?

Problem-solving abilities in infants can be seen as early as 69 months of age. They may attempt to manipulate objects to achieve a desired outcome, such as reaching for a toy or figuring out how to open a container.

How can I help my baby's cognitive development in the second year of life?

Offer age-appropriate puzzles, shape sorters, and stacking toys to encourage problem-solving and fine motor skills. Participate in activities that foster language acquisition, such as reading literature, performing melodies, and identifying objects in the surroundings.

When should I be concerned about my baby's sensory or cognitive development?

Suppose you notice significant delays or regressions in your baby's sensory or cognitive development, such as lack of responsiveness to sensory stimuli, limited exploration, or difficulty reaching developmental milestones. In that case, it's essential to discuss your concerns with a pediatrician or early intervention specialist for further evaluation and support.

How do infants develop their sense of object permanence, and when does this typically emerge?

Object permanence, the realization that things persist even when we can't see them, usually starts to show up between 8 and 12 months of age. Babies learn this concept through playing hide-and-seek with things over and over again.

What role does sensory integration play in infants' cognitive development?

Integrating information from several senses to create a cohesive perception is an essential part of growing up cognitively. It helps infants make sense of their surroundings, learn about cause and effect, and develop concepts such as size, shape, and texture.

How can I support my baby's sensory development through everyday activities?

Participate in pursuits that arouse a variety of senses, such as providing opportunities for tactile exploration with textured toys or fabrics, introducing various scents and flavors during mealtime, and playing music or singing songs to enhance auditory stimulation.

When do infants begin to demonstrate imitation skills, and why is this crucial for cognitive development?

Infants may start to demonstrate imitation skills as early as 69 months of age, such as copying gestures or facial expressions. Imitation is vital for cognitive development as it helps babies learn from others, understand social cues, and acquire new skills through observation and practice.

What are some signals that my infant is developing problem-solving abilities?

Signs that your baby is developing problem-solving abilities include trying multiple techniques to attain a goal, employing trial and error to tackle simple problems, and displaying persistence when presented with hurdles.

How can symbolic play assist cognitive development in toddlers?

Symbolic play, which includes believing one object represents another (e.g., using a block as a phone), helps children develop symbolic thinking and language skills. It increases creativity, inventiveness, and the ability to portray abstract topics.

What role does memory play in newborns' cognitive development, and when do memory skills usually emerge?

Memory plays a critical function in cognitive development by allowing newborns to retain and recall knowledge from past experiences. Memory skills usually emerge during the second half of the first year, with newborns displaying recognition memory and later gaining the ability to recall events or patterns.

How can I create a secure and exciting environment to help my baby's sensory and cognitive development?

Give the kids a wide range of age-appropriate playthings and sensory items to discover. Ensure that the setting is free from risks and allows chances for safe exploration and sensory experiences.

What are some ways to improve language development through sensory play?

Engage in activities that entail sensory experiences while adding language-rich interactions, such as expressing feelings (e.g., "This feels soft and squishy") or naming objects and actions (e.g., "Look at the red ball bouncing").

When should I seek expert help if I have concerns about my baby's sensory or cognitive development?

Suppose you have concerns about your baby's sensory or cognitive development, such as persistent delays, regression, or strange behaviors. In that case, it's vital to talk with a doctor or early intervention specialist for assessment and direction on suitable measures.

Chapter Three

Health, medicine, and treatment stages of newborns

What can I anticipate from my baby's first pediatrician visit, and when should I make the appointment?

It is advisable to arrange for your infant's initial pediatrician appointment during the initial week following delivery. Your pediatrician will examine your child thoroughly, evaluate their growth and development, and address any concerns you may have regarding feeding and sleeping during this visit.

In the first two years of life, which vaccinations is my child required, and when should they have them?

For protection against dangerous infections, your infant will require many vaccinations during the first two years of life. DTaP, IPV, Hib, PCV13, RV, and Hepatitis B are a few of these vaccines. You will receive a vaccination schedule from your pediatrician that details the recommended times for each shot.

What are some frequent ailments and diseases that babies may face during their first two years of life?

Infants frequently suffer from ear infections, fevers, thrush, diaper rash, and colds. It's critical to keep a careful eye on your baby's symptoms and speak with your pediatrician if you have any worries about their health or welfare.

What is the best way to comfort my ill or uncomfortable baby?

When your baby is sick or unhappy, you may help them feel better by giving them comfort measures like cuddles, soft rocking, using a humidifier to reduce congestion, and making sure they drink plenty of water. Only a pediatrician should be consulted before administering over-the-counter drugs.

When should I take my infant to the doctor if they are sick or exhibiting symptoms?

In the event that your infant's core temperature rises above 100.4°F (38°C), has trouble breathing, exhibits indications of dehydration, or you have concerns about their symptoms or behavior, you should take them to the doctor.

How can I make teething more comfortable for my baby?

By giving your infant teething toys or rings to gnaw on, gently massaging their gums with a clean finger, providing relaxed or chilled teething rings, or utilizing over-the-counter teething gels or medications under a pediatrician's supervision, you can help lessen your baby's discomfort during teething.

How should I respond if my child inadvertently swallows something poisonous?

If you think your child may have consumed something poisonous, call poison control right away or go to the emergency room. Be ready to offer details about the chemical consumed and keep the poison control phone number close at hand.

How do I make sure my child gets the suitable medical attention and care?

Make sure your child receives the proper medical care by making time for routine checkups with their pediatrician, according to the advised immunization schedule, and getting help right away if you have any concerns about your child's health or development.

Which typical first aid methods for infants should I be familiar with?

It's critical to understand how to treat scrapes, burns, and bug bites with basic first aid as well as newborn CPR and choking signals. To acquire these vital abilities, think about enrolling in a course in infant CPR and first aid.

What are some safe practices for giving my baby medicine?

Always give medication in accordance with your pediatrician's recommendations and the recommended dosage. Syringes or droppers are suitable measuring tools. Do not give medication meant for older children or adults to infants.

How can I shield my infant from common infections and illnesses that affect children?

By maintaining proper hygiene, which includes often washing your hands, making sure your child has had all of their vaccines, and avoiding close contact with sick people wherever possible, you may help prevent ordinary children's diseases and infections.

How should I respond if my child reacts adversely to a vaccine?

Although vaccination reactions are uncommon, call your pediatrician right away if your child has any side effects, including fever, edema, or rash. Although the majority of responses are mild and go away on their own, your physician can offer advice on how to manage symptoms.

How can I take care of my baby's oral health, and when should they start seeing a dentist?

Upon the emergence of their first tooth or by their first birthday, whichever comes first, your infant should visit the dentist. When teeth erupt, one can effectively maintain their dental well-being by employing a soft-bristled toothbrush and fluoride toothpaste for tooth brushing, alongside the practice of cleansing their gums with a clean, moistened towel subsequent to meals.

How should I respond if my child has a diaper rash?

In the event that your child has a diaper rash, protect the skin by applying a barrier cream or ointment, changing diapers often, and keeping the region clean and dry. Wipes and other products with alcohol or scents should not be used on sensitive skin.

How can I ease my infant's discomfort while they are sick, such as when they cough or have congestion?

By placing a cool-mist humidifier in your baby's room, giving them saline nasal sprays to help clear their nasal passages, and by ensuring adequate hydration through regular water intake, individuals can alleviate symptoms of congestion or coughing.

What are the telltale indicators of an ear infection in my kid, and when should I have them checked out?

Baby ear infections can be identified by straining or tugging at the ear, fussiness or irritability, fever, and trouble sleeping. See your pediatrician for an evaluation and course of treatment if you think your child may have an ear infection or if they show any of these symptoms.

How much fluoride should my infant be supplemented with, and when should they start?

If you live in a place where the water isn't fluoridated, or if your child's pediatrician suggests it because they risk tooth decay, your child might benefit from taking supplements of fluoride. The proper dosage will vary based on your baby's age and the level of fluoride in your water.

What should I do if my infant throws up or has diarrhea?

Make sure your baby stays hydrated if they vomit or have diarrhea by giving them short, frequent feedings of breast milk, formula, or oral rehydration solution. If symptoms deteriorate or if you see signs of dehydration, such as reduced urine production or dry mouth, it is advisable to seek medical assistance.

How can I shield my child from common allergies and sensitivities that affect children?

By gently and one at a time introducing potentially allergenic foods, like peanuts and eggs, to your infant and keeping an eye out for any adverse reactions, you can help protect them against common allergies and sensitivities. For advice on preventing allergies, speak with your pediatrician if allergies run in your family.

When does a feverish baby warrant medical attention, and what steps should I take to soothe them?

If your infant has a fever, keep an eye on their temperature and look out for any additional signs like rash, drowsiness, or trouble breathing. Seek medical assistance right away if your kid, who is less than three months old, attains or exceeds a rectal temperature of 100.4°F (38°C). For advice on how to treat a fever in older infants and when to seek emergency treatment, speak with your pediatrician.

What are some typical signs of baby dehydration, and how can I avoid it?

Dehydrated infants frequently have sunken eyes, dry mouths, decreased urine production, and sedentary behavior. Making sure your infant gets enough fluids, such as breast milk, formula, or oral rehydration solution, especially in hot weather or during illness, can help prevent dehydration.

How can I give my infant over-the-counter medication safely?

Always give your baby over-the-counter drugs according to the dosage recommendations on the container or as directed by your pediatrician to ensure safety. Don't give newborns adult dosages or prescriptions; instead, use syringes or droppers, which are suitable measuring tools.

When should I start giving my infant solid foods, and how can I be sure they're getting enough nutrition?

At six months of age, your baby can begin receiving solid foods, as advised by the American Academy of Pediatrics. Start your baby off with iron-fortified cereals made from a single component, then go on to pureed fruits, veggies, and meats. To guarantee that your infant gets the nutrients they need for healthy growth and development, provide a range of nutrient-dense foods.

How can I assist my infant to feel better if they are constipated, and what should I do?

If your infant is constipated, you can assist in easing their discomfort by giving them lots of fluids (water, diluted fruit juice, etc.) and high-fiber meals (puréed peas, prunes, etc.). Cycling leg motions and a light abdominal massage may also encourage bowel motions.

When can I begin sleep training my infant, and how can I help them form healthy sleeping habits?

Establishing a regular bedtime routine, making your baby's sleep environment peaceful and comforting, and attending to their cues for sleep are all ways to help your baby develop healthy sleep habits. When your baby is between 4 and 6 months old, you can apply sleep training techniques like gradual extinction or fading. However, the best course of action will depend on your baby's particular needs, so speak with your pediatrician.

What should I do in the event that my child gets an allergic rash or has a medication reaction?

Should your child exhibit an adverse reaction to a drug or break out in an allergic rash, cease giving the medication right once and get in touch with your pediatrician for additional assessment and advice. Your pediatrician could advise stopping the drug or trying a different course of therapy.

How can I aid in my child's recovery from a respiratory ailment or common cold?

By making sure your baby gets enough sleep, staying hydrated, using a cool mist humidifier to reduce congestion, and by employing a bulb syringe or nasal aspirator to meticulously extract mucus from their nose, you can improve their recuperation from a common cold or respiratory infection.

What are some indicators that my infant might have a food allergy, and when should I get in touch with a doctor?

A food allergy in newborns may manifest as hives, swelling, vomiting, diarrhea, or trouble breathing soon after the meal is consumed. You should speak with your pediatrician for additional assessment, diagnosis, and treatment if you think your child may have a food allergy.

When my kid starts eating solid foods, how can I support them in creating good eating habits?

Offering a range of wholesome meals, setting an example of good eating habits, and setting up a distraction-free, happy mealtime atmosphere are all ways you may support your baby's development of healthy eating habits. It is best to let your infant self-regulate how much food they consume rather than pressuring or forcing them to.

What are some crucial safety factors to take into account when giving medication to babies?

Always check the expiration date before using medication on newborns, store it safely out of reach, and never provide medication meant for adults or older children without first seeing your pediatrician. Never take more medication than is advised; always pay close attention to the dose directions.

Feeding and nutrition stages of infants

What are some suitable first meals to feed my baby, and when should I start them on solid foods?

Around six months of age, or when your baby begins to show signs of readiness, such as being able to sit up with assistance and displaying an interest in food, it is typically advised to start feeding them solid foods. The first foods that are appropriate for a baby are pureed fruits and vegetables (such as sweet potatoes and carrots) and infant cereals enriched with iron.

How often should I give my newborn a bottle or breast milk?

Typically, newborns require on-demand feedings, which could amount to up to 8 to 12 feedings every day. While formula-fed newborns may take in approximately 23 ounces of formula per meal during their first few weeks of life, breastfed babies may nurse every 23 hours.

What indicators are present to determine the readiness of my child to transition from formula or breast milk to solid foods?

When your baby shows interest in eating, can sit up with assistance, has decent head control, and Once the tongue-thrust reflex, the process entails expelling food from the oral cavity using the tongue, is no longer present, it is necessary to transition them to solid meals.

If my kid is fussy about food or refuses to eat certain things, how can I make sure they are getting enough nutrients?

Serve a range of nutrient-dense foods at every meal, and gradually add new items as well. It could take several exposures for your infant to accept a particular meal, so be persistent and patient. In order to discover what your baby prefers, you can also experiment with serving food in various formats, such as mashed, pureed, or finger foods.

What are some typical symptoms of dietary intolerances or allergies in babies, and what should I do if I think my child may have one?

Rash, hives, vomiting, diarrhea, and asthma are typical symptoms of food allergies or intolerances in babies. You should seek advice and examination from your pediatrician if you think your child may have a food allergy. To find the offending food, they could advise allergy testing or an elimination diet.

How can I properly introduce foods that cause allergies to my newborn, like eggs or peanuts?

One by one, in tiny portions, introduce allergenic foods and keep an eye out for any indications of an allergic reaction. If there is no reaction, you can start with a tiny taste and progressively increase the dosage over a few days. When you can keep a careful eye on your infant, such as throughout the day, it's a good idea to introduce these foods.

How can I assist my infant in developing healthy eating practices once they begin to consume solid foods?

Provide a range of nutrient-dense foods, set an example of good eating habits, and establish a distraction-free, happy dining atmosphere. Give your infant finger foods to self-feed in order to promote independence and let them experiment with flavors and textures at their leisure.

How can I make sure my growing infant is getting enough milk and nutrients while I am nursing them?

When your baby exhibits signs of hunger, like rooting or sucking on their hands, nurse them. To optimize milk transfer during breastfeeding sessions, make sure you are latching and positioned correctly. Keep an eye out for your baby's weight increase and wet diaper output as markers of sufficient milk consumption.

When is the right time to start giving my infant water or other drinks?

When your baby is about six months old, especially if they are eating solid foods and it's hot outside, you can introduce water to their diet. Steer clear of providing juice or other sweetened beverages since they may replace more nutrient-dense foods and add extra calories.

When is the appropriate time to switch my infant from breast milk or formula to whole cow's milk with no adverse effects?

Around the age of 12 months, most newborns can go from breast milk or formula to whole cow's milk if they are consuming a varied diet that includes other sources of calcium and minerals. Tolerating other dairy products and maintaining a varied diet rich in iron-rich foods are signs of preparation.

How can I determine whether my child is receiving enough formula or breast milk during feedings?

Contentment following feedings, consistent weight gain, the ability to produce multiple wet diapers per day, and reaching developmental milestones are indicators that your baby is receiving enough breast milk or formula. If you're worried, speaking with a pediatrician or lactation specialist will help ease your mind.

What are some tactics for managing eating difficulties like colic or reflux?

Keeping the baby upright after feedings and eating smaller, more frequent meals can be helpful in reducing the symptoms of reflux in infants. Offering a pacifier and softly rocking or swaying the infant during feedings might help soothe fussy babies. See your pediatrician for individual guidance.

When is it appropriate to start giving my kid solid meals that contain allergies, like peanuts or shellfish?

When a child is six months old, allergic foods like peanuts or shellfish can usually be introduced, as advised by medical professionals. Start with a tiny dosage and keep an eye out for any adverse effects. Before introducing foods that trigger allergies, speak with your pediatrician if there is a family history of the condition.

What are some telltale signals that my child is prepared to move from purees to foods with more extraordinary textures?

When you discover that your baby begin to sit up without support, shows interest in picking up substances and taking them into their mouth, and moves their tongue side to side to handle food, it is time for them to move on to more solid meals. To promote chewing and swallowing, you can progressively introduce softer, mashed meals and thicker purees.

How can I get my infant to prefer drinking from a cup over a bottle?

Your infant might develop accustomed to the idea of nursing or bottle-feeding by gradually being introduced to a cup. Give your infant tiny portions of water or breast milk/formula in an open cup or a handle-equipped sippy cup so they can experiment and practice drinking on their own.

What are some telltale signals that my child is prepared to transition from formula or breastfeeding?

A decrease in interest in nursing or bottle-feeding, a quick acceptance of solid meals and liquids, and self-soothing behaviors like cuddling or thumb-sucking are all indications that your baby could be ready to wean.

How can I get my infant to sample different foods and flavors?

Serve a range of foods, such as fruits, vegetables, cereals, and proteins, with different flavors and textures. Allow your infant to use their hands to investigate food, and promote self-feeding using finger foods. Having family dinners and setting an example of healthy eating practices can also promote experimental eating.

Are there any foods or medications that I should not give my infant in their first year of life?

Absolutely, keep your kid away from honey, cow's milk, and items like hard candies, nuts, and whole grapes that pose a choking threat. Reduce your intake of processed meals, added sugars, and salt. If there is a family history of allergies, proceed with caution while consuming certain foods.

In the first year of life, what impact does formula or nursing have on an infant's general nutrition and development?

During the first year of life, breastfeeding or formula feeding boosts an infant's growth and development by providing vital nutrients and antibodies. Even after solid meals are introduced, breast milk or formula should be the child's primary source of nutrition until the child is about 12 months old.

In particular, if my child is exclusively breastfed, how can I make sure they are getting enough iron in their diet?

Serve meals high in iron, such as lentils, beans, pork, chicken, and fish, as well as iron-fortified cereals. Additionally, as vitamin C improves the absorption of iron, you can include foods high in vitamin C, such as fruits and vegetables. You should speak with a qualified dietitian or your pediatrician if you are worried about your baby's iron intake.

Comfort and teething phases of an infant's growth

When will my kid begin to erupt teeth?

Although it varies greatly from child to infant, teething usually starts at six months of age. While some kids may begin teething as early as 3 to 4 months of age, others might not start until they are almost a year old.

What common symptoms can I look out for if my kid is teething?

Increased drooling, biting on objects, irritation, swollen or sore gums, disturbed sleep patterns, and appetite loss are typical symptoms of teething.

How can I ease my baby's discomfort during teething?

To relieve swollen gums, give your baby icy teething toys or washcloths, give them rings to chew on, gently massage their gums with a clean finger, and give them cold foods like yogurt or purees.

Is it safe to give my infant medication or teething gels to ease the discomfort associated with teething?

Before using any teething gels or pills, speak with your pediatrician. Certain products may contain substances that are dangerous for young children. In certain situations, over-the-counter analgesics like ibuprofen or baby acetaminophen may be advised.

What should I do if my kid is drooling excessively or if teething is causing skin irritation?

Apply a light barrier lotion to protect your baby's skin, and always have a clean cloth on hand to wipe up extra drool. To keep your infant dry and comfortable, use bibs that are soft and absorbent.

If teething is keeping my baby from sleeping, how can I help them feel better?

Provide additional comfort and calming methods to aid in your baby's sleep restoration, such as rocking, hugging, or light massage. If your baby wakes up from teething discomfort, give them a cool, damp washcloth to chew on.

Are there any homeopathic or natural medications that can ease the discomfort associated with teething?

Some parents discover that their newborns get respite from natural therapies such as homeopathic teething tablets, herbal teething powders, and chamomile tea. But before attempting any alternative treatments, make sure you speak with a healthcare professional to be sure they are suitable and safe for your child.

Can teething produce symptoms other than sore gums?

While the gums are the main organ affected by teething, some newborns may also have modest symptoms, including low-grade fever, diarrhea, or mild rash. Consult a physician to eliminate alternative etiologies, though, if your child exhibits more severe symptoms or seems exceptionally ill.

How much time does it usually take for teething to occur?

Every baby's teething process is unique, but as each tooth erupts, it usually lasts anywhere from a few months to more than a year. Around age three, most infants will have lost all of their primary teeth.

When teething is over, what can I do to provide my kid stability and comfort?

After teething is over, keep providing stability and comfort by holding close, rocking gently, playing calming music, or using a cherished blanket or stuffed animal. A regular bedtime ritual can also aid in your baby's feeling safe and at ease before going to sleep.

Can my baby's continuous runny nose or cough be caused by teething?

Coughing or a runny nose are not directly caused by teething. But occasionally, drooling might come from your baby's increased salivation during teething, which can irritate their nose and throat and cause symptoms like a runny nose or cough. It's critical to keep an eye on your baby's symptoms and seek medical attention if they worsen or continue.

When teething, my baby seems to be in discomfort. What kind of help can I give them?

To ease your baby's discomfort during teething, provide comfort with soft hugging, rocking, or massage. Give your baby some cooled washcloths or teething toys to chew on, and if your baby is in a lot of pain, you may want to use over-the-counter medications that your pediatrician has advised.

Teething pain is keeping my kid up at night. How can I improve their quality of sleep?

Create a soothing bedtime ritual to aid in your baby's relaxation before bed. Provide a cool, moist towel or teething toy for them to gnaw on in case they wake up from teething discomfort. You may also provide comfort measures like rocking or light massage. For additional advice on how to handle teething-related sleep disruptions, speak with your pediatrician.

Teething has been linked to diarrhea, I've heard. Is this accurate?

Although some parents may see loose stools or a minor upset stomach during teething, there isn't much scientific proof that teething causes diarrhea. It's critical to keep an eye on your baby's fluid intake if they have diarrhea or other gastrointestinal symptoms and to seek medical attention if the symptoms get worse or persist.

Can my baby get a fever from teething?

A low-grade fever is sometimes associated with teething. Still, it's essential to check your baby's temperature and get medical assistance if the fever is high, persistent, or accompanied by other worrisome symptoms. It's critical to screen out other probable reasons for fever because it can also indicate a sickness unrelated to teething.

What should I do if my kid is teething and won't eat or drink?

Provide your infant with soft, manageable meals and urge them to drink water, formula, or breast milk to stay hydrated. If your baby isn't interested in eating, don't force them; instead, give them tiny, frequent meals and offer comfort and assurance while they're not eating.

During teething, my infant is quite grumpy and fussy. Is this typical?

It is true that during teething, babies often become fussier and more irritable due to discomfort and disturbed sleep habits. During this period, try different soothing tactics and provide comfort and support to help your infant feel safer and at ease.

If my infant doesn't seem to be teething right away, should I worry?

Infants' timing of teething can vary greatly, so it's not always a reason to be concerned if teething takes longer than expected. For additional assessment, speak with a pediatrician if your child has not begun teething by around 1215 months of age or if you have any other worries regarding their growth or dental health.

How can I make sure my kid is comfortable when teething is over?

Even after teething, give comfort and security by showing affection, delivering prompt care, and creating a loving environment. In order to foster emotions of safety and security in your kid, respond quickly to their demands, provide lots of cuddles and sound interactions, and keep up a regular schedule.

How can I help my infant feel better emotionally both during and after teething?

Give your infant consolation and confidence, pay attention to their indications right away, and create a secure, nurturing atmosphere in which they can explore and develop. Developing a close relationship with your infant via loving interactions and supportive parenting can support their emotional health and resilience.

Chapter Four

The emotional and attachment development phases of infants

Throughout the first year of life, how does an infant's emotional development progress?

Infants' emotional development moves from simple needs expressions, such as screaming because of hunger or discomfort, to more complex feelings like fear, excitement, and dissatisfaction. Babies gain social awareness and empathy as they discover how to identify and react to other people's feelings.

How can I help my infant develop a safe bond with me, and when do babies usually start displaying indications of attachment to caregivers?

In the first few months of life, babies frequently begin to develop attachments to their caregivers; around 68 months, there is a noticeable increase in attachment behaviors. By being attentive to your baby's needs, giving comfort and love, and interacting lovingly and responsively, you can help them develop a stable bond.

What are the telltale signals that show my baby is firmly bonded to me?

Indicators of a secure attachment include displaying confidence in exploring their environment while occasionally checking in with caregivers for reassurance, seeking consolation from caregivers when disturbed, making eye contact, and smiling in response to engagement.

How can I help my infant in the first year of life with their emotional development?

Assist your infant's emotional growth by creating a kind and accommodating atmosphere for them to be cared for, recognizing and validating their emotions, and providing consolation and assurance when they're in need. Play and have constructive conversations to make your relationship stronger.

What part do regular activities play in helping my infant develop emotional security?

Routines that are predictable and consistent, including eating, sleeping, and playing, give babies a sense of stability and security and improve their emotional health. Additionally, routines foster positive interactions and opportunities for connecting with caregivers.

How can I know if my baby's separation anxiety is typical, and how can I assist them in dealing with it?

Yes, separation anxiety is a joint emotional development that usually shows up at about 6 to 8 months of age. By introducing brief separations to your infant gradually, providing comfort and assurance, and upholding regular routines, you can help them learn to cope.

When I leave the room or meet new people, my infant shows indications of discomfort. What should I do?

When your infant is in distress, respond to them with compassion and assurance, recognizing their emotions and offering consolation and assistance. Allow them to acclimate at their rate as you gradually expose them to new situations and people.

How can I help my child feel safe and confident while interacting with other caregivers, such as grandparents or daycare centers?

Encourage frequent interactions, uphold regular routines in all caregiving settings, and make sure caregivers are sensitive to your baby's wants and emotions to cultivate strong relationships with other caregivers.

What possible impacts on my baby's emotional development could inconsistent caregiving or neglect have?

A baby's emotional development can be severely impacted by inconsistent caregiving or neglect, which can result in behavioral issues, attachment problems, and long-term emotional insecurity. Encouraging good emotional development requires caregiving that is attentive and consistent.

When should I get professional assistance if I'm worried about my baby's bonding or emotional growth?

If you're worried about your baby's behavior, connection, or emotional development, follow your gut and see your pediatrician. In order to address potential issues and encourage healthy emotional development, early intervention and support are helpful.

What part does responsive parenting play in promoting attachment and healthy emotional development?

Encouraging your baby's needs with empathy and attention is a crucial component of responsive parenting, which promotes safe connection and sound emotional development. Giving in to your baby's instincts quickly establishes a foundation of strong emotional attachments by making them feel secure and appreciated.

As my child gets older, how can I assist them learn to control their emotions?

When your baby is distressed, you can soothe them with gentle rocking, singing, or hugging to help them learn how to control their emotions. Encourage them to verbally communicate their emotions as their language skills grow, and give them validation for those feelings so they may learn to understand and control them.

One caregiver appears to be my baby's top choice over the others. Is this typical?

Indeed, it is not unusual for infants to express a preference for one primary caregiver, usually the one who gives them the most care. This preference may change over time as the baby's interactions change; it is a regular aspect of attachment development.

How can I help my infant emotionally develop as they get more self-sufficient and mobile?

As your infant gains mobility and independence, support their exploration and autonomy while continuing to provide comfort and security. Make sure they have a secure space to explore, and be there to support and encourage them as they try new things.

What are some indicators that my child is growing in social empathy?

Sharing toys or things with others, expressing comfort or worry when others are distressed, and displaying an awareness of others' feelings through gestures and facial expressions are all indications that your baby is growing in empathy.

If my kid is extremely clingy or refuses to be carried by others, should I be concerned?

Babies frequently experience moments of clinginess or fear around strangers as they form attachments and become more aware of their environment. Although you should respect your baby's need for comfort and familiarity, you should encourage a gradual introduction to new people and situations.

What are some methods for easing my baby's adjustment to new surroundings or caregivers?

Maintaining regular habits and offering dependable comfort items, like a cherished blanket or toy, can help ease transitions. Introduce your infant to new locations and caregivers gradually to give them time to become used to it while providing comfort and assurance.

How can I help my child form healthy friendships and social contacts as they get older?

Give your infant the chance to socialize with other children by enrolling them in playgroups, classes, or childcare facilities. Promote cooperation, sharing, and taking turns. Set a good example for others by acting in socially responsible ways.

How can I help my infant develop coping mechanisms and emotional resilience?

By creating a secure and caring atmosphere, encouraging problem-solving techniques, and assisting your child in gaining a sense of self-efficacy and control over their surroundings, you may support their emotional resilience.

When should I get professional help if I'm worried about my baby's bonding or emotional growth?

Consider seeking advice and support from a doctor, child psychologist, or other competent healthcare expert if you have ongoing worries about your baby's emotional development, attachment, or behavior that affects their day-to-day functioning or wellness.

Social and emotional development phases of infants

When do babies start displaying social skills like smiling and eye contact?

Social behaviors in infants usually start to emerge in the first few weeks of life. Early social engagement is indicated by the fact that they may begin to smile and make eye contact with familiar faces and voices.

What exactly are attachment behaviors, and when do babies usually start exhibiting them?

Infants who form a close emotional link with their primary caregivers are said to exhibit attachment behaviors. These behaviors usually start to show themselves between the ages of 6 and 8 months, when babies begin to respond more to their caregivers' presence and look to them for security and comfort.

How can I help my infant develop healthy social skills and attachment?

By using responsive and caring caregiving techniques, such as holding, caressing, and conversing with your infant, you can promote healthy social relationships and bonding with your child. Building trust and security in the caregiver-infant relationship is facilitated by swiftly attending to your baby's indications for comfort and attention.

What social development benchmarks are typical for the first year of life?

During the first year of life, smiling in response to others, chattering and cooing in response to interactions, displaying interest in social games like peekaboo, and expressing preference for familiar caregivers are typical milestones in social development.

When do babies usually start to show signs of empathy and emotional comprehension in others?

Between the ages of nine and twelve months, infants start to show signs of empathy and awareness of the feelings of others. In reaction to the suffering of others, they could display comfort or worry and begin to mimic motions and facial expressions to demonstrate empathy.

What part do playtime and peer contact play in the social development of infants?

Infants' social development is greatly aided by playtime and peer interaction, which teaches them communication, collaboration, and social conventions. Simple encounters with other babies or siblings can help infants learn emotional control and social awareness.

In what ways may I assist my child in developing emotionally?

During the toddler years, you may help your child's emotional development by giving them a secure and encouraging space to explore and express themselves, recognizing and validating their feelings, and teaching them age-appropriate coping mechanisms for handling their emotions.

What are some telltale indicators that my child is maturing emotionally and socially?

Cooperative play with peers, expressing a range of emotions, managing disappointment or frustration, and exhibiting empathy and understanding of others' feelings are all indications that your toddler is maturing socially and emotionally.

When is it appropriate for me to worry about my baby's emotional and social development?

Each kid develops at their rate, but if you observe chronic difficulties in building relationships, severe delays or regression in social or emotional milestones, or worrying behaviors like intense aggressiveness or withdrawal, you may want to speak with your pediatrician.

How can I help my kid develop a stable attachment relationship and a strong parent-child bond?

By being consistently and lovingly caring for your baby, being emotionally present and sensitive to their needs, and participating in good, interactive experiences that build trust and connection, you may help your baby develop a strong parent-child bond and a safe attachment relationship.

What are some techniques to support my infant's growth in self-control?

Establishing predictable routines, creating a peaceful and relaxing environment, comforting and reassuring your baby when they are in distress, and setting an example of composed and controlled behavior are all helpful strategies for assisting your baby in learning self-regulation.

At what age does a baby usually start exhibiting symptoms of stranger anxiety, and how can I assist them in managing it?

During 6 to 8 months of age, newborns start to notice unfamiliar faces and may get upset when they are among strangers. It is when stranger anxiety usually appears. By progressively introducing them to new people in comfortable environments and letting them approach others at their own pace, you may help your baby learn to deal with their fear of strangers.

How can I help my kid form healthy social relationships with peers or older siblings?

Provide opportunities for supervised play and contact, set an excellent example of gentle and cooperative behavior, promote sharing and taking turns, and acknowledge positive interactions and collaboration to foster positive social connections between your baby and older siblings or peers.

How can I foster in my child an awareness of other people's feelings and empathy?

By categorizing emotions during exchanges, offering chances for perspective-taking and role-playing, and setting an example of empathy in your relationships with others, you can aid your infant in developing empathy and knowledge of the feelings of others.

What part does attentive parenting play in the social and emotional development of young children?

By encouraging a sense of security, trust, and emotional control in your baby, responsive parenting, which entails quickly and sensitively reacting to your baby's indications for comfort and attention plays a critical role in their social and emotional development.

When do babies usually start acting assertively and independently in social situations?

Around 12 to 18 months of age, as they get more confident in their ability to move around and communicate, infants usually start to show signs of independence and assertiveness in their social interactions. Healthy independence can be fostered by supporting and guiding while also encouraging autonomy.

What are some methods for assisting my child in forming positive attachment bonds with other caregivers, such as grandparents or daycare centers?

Maintaining consistency in caregiving practices, promoting bonding through shared activities and rituals, and supporting gradual transitions between caregivers to minimize separation anxiety are some strategies for helping your baby develop healthy attachment bonds with other caregivers.

How can I encourage social development in my infant while they're playing?

During playtime, you may help your baby's social development by giving playdates or parent-child classes, which are chances for social interaction with peers; by providing age-appropriate toys and games that promote cooperation and sharing; and by setting an example of positive social behaviors.

What are some telltale indicators that my child is developing strong bonds with their caregivers?

When your baby seeks solace and assurance from familiar caregivers in times of distress, shows signs of pleasure and joy when they return, and shows a readiness to explore their surroundings when they feel safe, these are indications that your baby is developing secure attachments with caregivers.

When my child starts daycare or gets a new sibling, for example, how can I support them in adjusting to these changes and transitions in their social environment?

By establishing regular routines and reassuring your baby, introducing them to age-appropriate explanations and familiarization, and providing extra support and attention during moments of adjustment, you may assist your baby in managing transitions and changes in their social environment.

Language and communication developmental stages of infants

When do newborns usually begin to babble and make noises?

Babies usually begin to babble and make noises at 4 to 6 months of age. When they are first exploring their vocal abilities, they might repeatedly produce consonant-vowel combinations (e.g., "ba-ba-ba," "da-da-da").

How can I support my infant's language development in the first year of life?

Engage in frequent conversation with your infant, describe everyday events, and react to their vocalizations. Encourage imitation of sounds and gestures, sing songs, read aloud from books, and use essential, repetitive words and phrases.

When do newborns usually say their first words?

Although this can vary greatly, most babies say their first words around 10 to 14 months of age. "Mama," "dada," "bye-bye," "hi," "ball," "dog," or the names of familiar things or people in their surroundings are frequently used as first words.

What are some telltale signs that, despite not yet being able to speak, my baby is understanding language?

Reacting to their name, obeying basic commands (like "wave bye-bye," "give me the toy"), pointing to objects of interest, and demonstrating recognition of words or phrases are all indications that your baby is beginning to understand language.

How can I help my infant develop their language skills as they get closer to turning one?

Maintain your conversations, build on your infant's communication attempts, and introduce new words and ideas. To communicate meaning and to create opportunities for social interaction with peers and caregivers, use gestures, facial expressions, and intonation.

When is my baby's language development something to be concerned about?

It might be worthwhile to discuss your concerns with a pediatrician or speech-language pathologist if your baby is not babbling by 7 to 9 months, saying single words by 12 to 15 months, or using simple phrases by 18 to 24 months. Additionally, get help and evaluation if your child exhibits other developmental delay symptoms or loses previously learned language skills.

What impact does a baby's exposure to various languages have on their language development?

A baby's language development can be aided by early exposure to various languages, which may result in bilingual or multilingual proficiency. Babies are able to pick up multiple languages at once and are able to discriminate between them based on exposure.

What strategies can I employ to facilitate the progression of my infant's linguistic abilities from babble to verbal expression?

Maintain a language-rich environment, set an example of proper speech, and give your infant lots of chances to interact verbally. Kindly grant them access to a warm reception when they try to communicate, encourage them to take turns in discussions, and acknowledge their efforts.

What are some methods for encouraging language development in the course of regular activities and routines?

During meals, baths, and playtime, take advantage of the chance to engage in language-rich interactions. Encourage your baby to use gestures, sounds, and words to express their needs and preferences by labeling objects, describing actions, and posing open-ended questions.

When is it appropriate for me to get worried if my toddler is speaking challenging to understand?

Toddlers are typically incoherent in speech as they develop their articulation skills. But suppose by the time your toddler is two years old. In that case, their speech is still consistently hard to understand, or if they have trouble making certain sounds or stringing words together, you might want to have a speech-language pathologist evaluate them.

How can I use play to support my infant's language development?

Talk, sing, and use language-rich toys like picture books, shape sorters, and musical instruments in interactive play activities.

Pay attention to your baby's vocalizations, follow their lead, and use play to introduce new words and ideas.

What are some telltale signs that my child is prepared to begin communicating with gestures?

Encourage and respond to your baby's early gestures to support their communication development. Some signs that your baby is ready to start using gestures are reaching to be picked up, pointing to objects of interest, waving goodbye, and shaking their head to indicate "no."

When can I anticipate that my infant will begin to comprehend basic instructions?

Around 8 to 12 months of age, babies usually start to comprehend basic commands like "Come here" or "Give me the toy." To make instructions easier for your baby to understand, use simple gestures, visual cues, and straightforward language.

How can I encourage my infant's language development while performing daily tasks like putting on clothes and changing diapers?

Take advantage of routines to engage in language-rich interactions. When changing diapers or dressing, label the body parts, articles of clothing, and movements. To help your baby develop vocabulary and comprehension skills, explain what you're doing, pose straightforward questions, and have conversations with them.

What are some tactics to help babies develop early literacy skills?

Regularly read to your infant beginning at birth. Select board books for young readers with straightforward, vibrant illustrations and exciting textures. Make animal sounds, point to pictures, and prod your child to turn the pages. As your child gets older, engage them in interactive storytelling by asking open-ended questions about the narrative.

In case my baby doesn't speak yet, how can I help them develop their language skills?

Promote nonverbal communication by using your body language, gestures, and facial expressions. When your baby makes vocalizations or attempts at communication, give them encouragement and enthusiasm in return. Repetition, imitation, and modeling are helpful tools for teaching your baby new words and sounds.

What part does providing attentive care have in fostering language development?

Being receptive to your baby's cues and signals and promptly and sensitively attending to their needs are all part of responsive caregiving. A loving and encouraging environment fosters meaningful interactions that advance language development and fortify the link between parents and children.

How can teaching sign language to my infant improve their communication skills? When should I start?

Around 68 months of age, when your baby starts expressing an interest in communication and is growing the motor skills necessary to make gestures, is when you can start teaching them the basics of sign language. Reduced frustration, early communication, and the development of spoken language are all aided by sign language.

What are some tactics for encouraging language acquisition in households with multiple languages?

Introduce your infant to all of the languages that are spoken in your home on a regular basis through books, rhymes, songs, and daily interactions. Give your infant a chance to engage with people who talk about each language, and through regular and purposeful exposure, encourage their bilingual or multilingual proficiency.

How can I keep an eye on my baby's milestones and language development?

Document your infant's language development in a journal or milestone tracker by noting their initial sounds, babbling, and first words. If your baby's language development worries you, consult developmental checklists and get advice from a speech-language pathologist or your pediatrician.

Chapter Five

Stages of sleep and rest that infants experience

What is the recommended sleep duration for a baby, and how often should they nap?

With naps included, newborns usually sleep for 14 to 17 hours a day. Nevertheless, they frequently get only a few hours of sleep every day. Because they require frequent rest to support their rapid growth and development, newborns may nap once every twelve hours.

When will my kid be able to sleep through the night?

Typically, infants begin to experience prolonged periods of nocturnal slumber between the ages of 3 and 6 months. Every infant is unique, though, and some can take longer to establish regular sleep habits than others. In promoting longer nights of sleep, it's critical to have a regular bedtime routine and healthy sleep habits.

What are some methods for assisting my infant in creating a regular sleep schedule?

To let your baby know when it's time to go to sleep, establish a regular bedtime ritual that includes things like washing, reading a story, and turning down the lights. Make the space peaceful for sleeping by keeping it quiet, dark, and at a pleasant temperature. While your baby is still awake but tired, put them to sleep to help them develop self-soothing abilities.

If my infant is having trouble falling asleep throughout the day, what should I do?

When your baby exhibits signs of exhaustion, such as wiping their eyes or fussing, try to put them down for a nap before they go too far. To help manage your baby's sleep patterns, create a nap-friendly environment by reducing noise and distraction and implementing a regular nap schedule.

Are my baby's sleep regressions ordinary, and if so, how can I handle them?

Yes, sleep regressions are typical in babies at several developmental periods, including between 4 and 12 months of age. These regressions could be brought on by regular adjustments, teething, or developmental milestones. In order to deal with sleep regressions, stick to a regular bedtime schedule, console and reassure your child, and exercise patience while they get used to their new sleep schedule.

When is the right time to move my child from a crib to a toddler bed?

Between the ages of 18 months and three years, most kids make the switch from a crib to a toddler bed, depending on their unique development and readiness. Climbing out of the crib or expressing interest in a big-kid bed are indications that your child could be ready for a toddler bed.

What are some strategies for calming my infant back to sleep and dealing with nighttime awakenings?

When your baby wakes up throughout the night, respond to them quickly but quietly, providing them with consolation and assurance without overstimulating them. Don't switch on bright lights or engage in stimulating activities at night, and limit your nocturnal contact. To help your baby fall back asleep, offer a comfort object, like a pacifier or a lovey.

How can I help my infant develop sound sleeping practices as they become toddlers?

Uphold regular sleep patterns and routines, give careful consideration to creating a peaceful sleeping environment, and set an example of good sleep hygiene. Promote self-soothing practices and progressively move away from sleep associations, such as rocking or breastfeeding to sleep, to foster independent sleep skills.

What are some telltale indicators of a sleep issue in my kid, and when should I get help from a professional?

Infants who have sleep disorders may exhibit odd sleep habits, excessive daytime sleepiness, trouble falling or staying asleep, or numerous night awakenings. See your pediatrician for an assessment and recommendations on what to do next if you think your child may have a sleep condition.

How can I balance my baby's sleep needs with my own need for relaxation and well-being as a parent?

Make self-care a priority by asking friends, relatives, or partners for help in splitting up caregiving duties and scheduling time off. Whenever possible, engage in relaxation techniques such as deep breathing or meditation to alleviate tension and promote restful sleep.

At what developmental stages does my baby require how many hours of sleep?

Depending on their age, babies require different amounts of sleep. The average number of hours a newborn sleeps per day is 14 to 17; this gradually drops to about 12 to 15 by 3 to 6 months and 11 to 14 hours by 6 to 12 months. With naps included, toddlers usually require 11 to 14 hours of sleep per night.

What are some typical sleep issues that babies might encounter, and how can I help them?

Infants often struggle with falling asleep, waking up during the night, and taking short naps. Establish a regular bedtime schedule, make your home sleep-friendly, and react quickly to your baby's sleep cues in order to overcome these difficulties. Furthermore, take into account sleep training techniques that suit the temperament and age of your infant.

What are several approaches that can be utilized, and at what point in time should sleep training be initiated for infants?

When your baby is developmentally ready, which is around 4 to 6 months old, you can begin sleep-training them. Weissbluth's method (extinction), the Ferber method (gradual extinction), and the "pick-up-put-down" method are a few sleep training techniques. Selecting a technique that fits both your parenting style and your child's temperament is crucial.

How can I start my baby off with good sleep habits at a young age?

Creating a regular sleep schedule, offering a peaceful and comforting sleeping environment, and teaching your infant to self-soothe are all essential steps in developing healthy sleep habits. Encourage your baby to learn how to fall asleep on their own by putting them to sleep while still awake but drowsy.

Are my baby's sleep regressions ordinary, and if so, how can I handle them?

Indeed, during times of rapid developmental changes, like those that occur at four months, 8 to 10 months, and 18 months, sleep regressions are ordinary. Sleep regressions can be managed by keeping your baby's sleep schedule consistent, providing extra comfort and assurance during times when they are more awake, and exercising patience as they adjust to new developmental milestones.

What effect does a nap during the day have on my baby's general quality of sleep?

Taking naps during the day is crucial for your baby's overall sleep health because it prevents overtiredness and encourages deeper sleep at night. Aim for age-appropriate nap times, and make sure your infant naps in a regular, sleep-friendly space that promotes healthy sleep.

When should my baby go from taking many naps during the day to taking fewer naps?

Around 6 to 9 months of age, most babies switch from taking three naps a day to two naps, and around 12 to 18 months, they switch from taking two naps a day to one nap. Depending on the particular sleep needs and patterns of your baby, the timing of the transition may change.

How can I help my baby transition between time zones or with daylight saving changes?

Your baby's sleep schedule should be gradually shifted by 15 to 30 minutes each day leading up to daylight saving time changes or time zones traveled. Continue to expose them to natural light and follow regular bedtime routines to aid in regulating their internal body clock.

What are some telltale signs that my infant is sleeping well and sufficiently?

Having regular sleep patterns, meeting developmental milestones on time, and waking up alert and rested are all indications that your baby is getting enough good sleep. Your baby should also be able to self-soothe back to sleep if they wake up during the night and have a regular sleep schedule.

When should I bring my baby's sleep issues to the attention of a healthcare provider?

See your pediatrician or a pediatric sleep specialist for an assessment and advice if you are concerned about your baby's sleep issues, including excessive daytime sleepiness, irregular sleep behaviors, or persistent nighttime waking.

Stages of development of infants' sleep patterns and routines

For the first year of their lives, how much sleep does my infant require?

The average number of hours a newborn sleeps every day is roughly 16 to 18, which gradually drops to 12 to 16 by 4 to 6 months and 11 to 14 by 9 to 12 months. With naps included, toddlers typically require 11 to 14 hours of sleep every day.

When will my kid be able to sleep through the night?
Typically, infants begin to experience prolonged periods of nocturnal slumber between the ages of 3 and 6 months. It's essential to keep in mind, too, that "sleeping through the night" could mean different things to different babies and doesn't always equate to eight hours without waking.

How do I get my infant into a sleep routine?
Create a regular sleep ritual that consists of soothing pursuits like reading, taking a bath, or soft rocking. To let your infant know when it's time to wind down and get ready for bed, stick to a basic, relaxing routine.

What actions should I take if my newborn experiences frequent nocturnal awakenings or encounters difficulty initiating sleep?
When your baby struggles to fall asleep or wakes up during the night, give them comfort and certainty. Assess for hunger, pain, or other needs, and act quickly to provide comfort using patting, rocking, or soft shushing.

Do my baby's erratic sleep habits, like short naps and numerous nighttime awakenings, make sense?

It is common for babies to experience erratic sleep habits, particularly in the initial months of their lives. The sleep habits of infants may exhibit increased regularity as they progress in age, but they may still experience fluctuations in the length of their sleep and the frequency of their wakefulness.

When is the right time to move my infant from several naps throughout the day to one continuous nap?

Between 6 to 9 months of age, most newborns go from taking several short naps to a single, consolidated sleep schedule consisting of one or two lengthier naps per day. When necessary, gently modify your baby's nap schedule based on their cues.

What are some techniques for assisting my infant in learning to comfort themselves and go to sleep on their own?

Give your infant opportunities to experience falling asleep on their own to promote self-soothing. One way to do this is to put them in their crib when they are sleepy but not yet asleep. When necessary, provide consolation and assurance, but gradually help your infant learn how to lull themselves to sleep.

If my infant has sleep regressions or disturbances throughout specific developmental stages, should I be concerned?

Sleep regressions are standard and typically transient, occurring around developmental milestones like teething or acquiring new abilities. While you know that your sleep habits will probably improve with time, stick to a regular sleep schedule and provide more comfort and support during these times.

What signals indicate that my child is prepared to go from a crib to a toddler bed?

Climbing out of the crib, exhibiting discomfort or resistance to being confined, or displaying an interest in a "big kid" bed are all indications that your baby could be ready for a toddler bed. When it seems secure and comfortable for your infant to go into a toddler bed, it's time.

How can I help my infant develop sound sleeping patterns as they grow into toddlers?

In order to establish clear sleep expectations, a consistent bedtime and nap schedule and a sleep-friendly atmosphere are all ways to encourage healthy sleep habits. Supporting your child's sleep development might involve encouraging positive connections with sleep and offering comfort and reassurance when needed.

What effect do my baby's length and frequency of daytime naps have on how well they sleep at night?

Taking naps during the day can affect your baby's nocturnal sleep and add to their overall sleep needs. Taking enough naps during the day might assist avoid becoming overtired, which promotes better quality sleep at night.

In order to keep my baby's sleep routine regular, should I wake him up from a nap?

Setting up a regular nap schedule is essential, but usually speaking, you don't need to wake your baby up from their naps. If your baby's ability to fall asleep at nighttime isn't significantly affected, let them finish their nap.

How can I make my baby's environment conducive to sleep?

Make sure the room is quiet, dark, and at a pleasant temperature to promote sleep. To block off light and reduce outside noise, use blackout drapes or white noise machines or fans.

What indicates that my child is prepared for a nap?

Your baby may be ready to stop naps if they are constantly refusing to go to sleep, taking longer to fall asleep during naps, or having trouble going to sleep at night because they are getting too much sleep during the day.

How can I help my baby transition between time zones or with daylight saving changes?

Prior to the time change or trip, gradually modify your baby's sleep routine by moving nap and bedtime timings by 15 minutes at a time. When your infant is awake, expose them to natural light to help them with internal clock regulation.

What should I do if my infant has trouble falling back asleep or wakes up a lot during the night?

Take care of any potential reasons for night terrors, such as hunger, pain, or links with sleep. Use calming methods to help your baby go back to sleep, like patting, soft rocking, or providing a pacifier.

How should I respond to illnesses or teething that interfere with my sleep?

Give teething toys or frozen teething rings as comfort and pain alleviation for teething discomfort. Whenever your baby's sleep schedule is disturbed by an illness, make the necessary adjustments and provide them with more comfort and care.

Is it acceptable to teach my kid to self-soothe using sleep training techniques?

Some families may find success with sleep training techniques, but it's essential to use caution and adjust the methods to your baby's temperament and developmental stage. For advice on safe and efficient sleep training methods, speak with a pediatrician or sleep specialist.

How can I keep my baby's sleep schedule consistent when they go to daycare or childcare?

Together, you may create a regular sleep pattern that suits your baby's needs by sharing your baby's sleep schedule and preferences with caregivers. To encourage comfort and familiarity during sleep periods, provide comfort items from home.

When should I think about getting professional assistance if my sleep problems are getting worse?

Should you have exhausted all possible remedies for your infant's sleep problems or if sleep disturbances have a substantial adverse influence on your baby's general health or day-to-day functioning, you might want to seek additional assessment and advice from a doctor or sleep specialist.

Chapter Six

Phases of discipline development in newborns

When should I begin training my child in discipline?
As early as infancy, discipline should start with gentle supervision and redirection. Even if it might not comprehend discipline in the conventional sense, routines, and boundaries can be established with the support of loving and persistent supervision.

Which disciplinary techniques work best for babies under a year old?
For infants younger than a year old, emphasize modeling good behavior, providing positive reinforcement, and using gentle redirection. Provide a secure atmosphere, swiftly attend to their requirements, and set up dependable routines.

How can I establish boundaries and restrictions for my child without using punishment?
Establishing boundaries and limits entails establishing a supportive atmosphere with precise expectations. When your kid exhibits undesirable behavior, refocus their attention and

use straightforward, consistent language. Reward good behavior with encouragement and praise.

When should I begin using the word "no" to my infant, and is it OK to say no?

Saying "no" to your infant when it's required is acceptable, but only in small, controlled doses. Around 6 to 9 months old, begin teaching the word; however, instead of using punishment, pair it with redirection or distraction.

How can I deal with my baby's tantrums or challenging behavior?

Babies frequently throw tantrums to express their feelings and make their independence known. Remain composed, comfort others, and impose reasonable boundaries. Give your infant a secure environment in which to vent their emotions and teach them constructive coping mechanisms.

When my child gets closer to toddlerhood, what are some telltale signals that they're ready for more rigid discipline?

When your infant can follow basic commands, shows a greater understanding of cause and effect, and wants independence, it's time for more structured discipline. Make a gradual transition to age-appropriate methods of discipline.

How can I use positive reinforcement to help my kids behave in the ways that I want them to?

Give your infant hugs, kisses, and other positive reinforcement when they behave in the desirable ways. Honor accomplishments and landmarks, no matter how minor, to support constructive behavior.

What should I do if, in spite of redirection, my kid persists in doing undesirable behaviors?

If redirection doesn't work, think about making environmental changes to reduce the likelihood of undesirable behavior being triggered. When rerouting, provide options and enforce boundaries consistently.

Is there a way to discipline my infant without hitting them?

Steer clear of physical punishment and instead concentrate on providing proper modeling, constructive criticism, and gentle direction. Physical punishment may not be an effective way to teach desirable behaviors and may even damage the parent-child bond.

When should I consult a professional to help me discipline my child?

Consulting with a pediatrician, child psychologist, or parenting coach can help if you're feeling overwhelmed, having trouble controlling your baby's behavior, or encountering recurrent issues. They can provide resources, support, and guidance to help you deal with the difficulties of raising a child.

How can I consistently discipline my baby?

When developing discipline procedures, consistency is essential. Establish precise guidelines and standards, then consistently enforce them. To give your baby structure, follow set eating, sleeping, and playtime routines.

How does positive reinforcement fit into the process of disciplining babies?

Discipline must include positive reinforcement since it promotes desired behaviors by rewarding them with tiny gifts, affection, or praise. It improves the parent-child bond and serves to reinforce positive conduct.

How can I use discipline to teach my infant the idea of cause and effect?

When rerouting your baby's behavior, employ essential cause-and-effect explanations. If they toss food on the ground, for instance, gently inform them that it signifies the end of mealtime. Enforcing punishments consistently aids in newborns' learning of the correlation between their behaviors and results.

Should I use timeouts as a means of discipline with my infant?

Infants under the age of one year old typically do not benefit from timeouts since they may not comprehend the idea. Instead, give careful consideration to positive reinforcement and redirection. When your child becomes older, roughly 18 to 24 months, you can use timeouts as a tool to help teach self-regulation.

How do I punish my child without compromising their independence?

Give your infant choices, but only within reason, to honor their developing independence. Saying something like, "Would you like to wear the blue shoes or the red shoes?" empowers your child while maintaining boundaries, as opposed to telling them to put on their shoes right now.

If my infant starts acting aggressively, like biting or hitting, what should I do?

React to violent behavior with composure but firmness by softly telling them "No" and guiding their focus to something more suitable to do. Set a calm example and provide ways for them to vent their frustrations or enthusiasm, such as squeezing a plush toy or taking deep breaths.

How can I use discipline to teach my infant how to control their emotions?

When your infant is upset, cuddle them and acknowledge their feelings. Urge them to use gestures or words to communicate how they are feeling. Teach children basic coping mechanisms as they get older, such as deep breathing or pausing when they feel overwhelmed.

When my baby pushes limits, is that normal, and how should I react?

Yes, as babies explore their surroundings and learn to be independent, they will inevitably challenge limits. When someone tests your boundaries, respond to them in a composed and consistent manner. Set clear but reasonable boundaries and assist as needed.

Should I give my infant treats or incentives to promote good behavior?

Bribery should not be used as a tool of manipulation, even though infrequent rewards can help to reinforce beneficial conduct. Instead, teach your infant desirable habits by emphasizing natural consequences and positive reinforcement.

How can I apply discipline and still have a good parent-child relationship?

Prioritize developing a close relationship with your child by providing responsive, loving care. Spend quality time together, be empathetic, and communicate honestly. Discipline becomes more respectful and effective when it is maintained in a loving and supporting relationship.

Developmental phases of newborns and parenting

How can my newborn and I bond?

Developing a close bond with your newborn is crucial to creating a robust attachment. Spend time stroking, holding, and conversing with your child. As babies cry, they quickly tend to their needs by giving them food, changing their diapers, and providing comfort.

Why is responsive parenting necessary, and what does it entail?

Responding to your baby's demands in a timely and considerate manner is part of being a responsive parent. This methodology cultivates a stable bond, advances sound emotional growth, and establishes the groundwork for favorable parent-child dynamics.

How can I help my child grow emotionally?

Offer lots of love and pleasant interactions, create a caring and responsive caregiving atmosphere, and acknowledge and respect your baby's feelings and emotions. Show compassion and understanding when you react to their indications and messages.

Which techniques work well for calming a fussy baby?

To soothe a cranky infant, try singing, swaddling, soft rocking, or employing white noise. Provide skin-to-skin contact, breastmilk, or bottle-feeding as a means of comfort, and observe your baby's unique calming preferences.

Why is tummy time essential, and what does it entail?

During tummy time, you should place your awake, supervising infant on their stomach. It encourages motor development, lessens the chance of flat spots developing on the back of the head, and strengthens the muscles in the arms, shoulders, and neck.

How can I help my infant develop their linguistic skills?

Talk to your infant all day long, read books to them together, explain your actions and surroundings, and engage in frequent verbal conversations. React excitedly and supportively to your baby's coos, babbles, and communication efforts.

How important is playtime for my baby's development?
Your baby's cognitive, social, and emotional development depend on play. Give them toys and activities that are appropriate for their age that will pique their curiosity and foster creativity, problem-solving, and exploration.

How can I help my infant develop sound sleeping habits?
Implement a consistent bedtime routine to communicate to your infant the appropriate time to retire for the night. Establish a serene and peaceful resting environment by reducing the brightness of the lights and introducing white noise or soft music. Promote the adoption of self-soothing skills and promptly respond to the sleep signs exhibited by your infant.

As a parent, what should I do if I feel overburdened or under pressure?
It's common for parents to have moments of overwhelm or tension. Ask for assistance from the people in your support system, such as friends, family, or partners. If you're having trouble overcoming chronic stress or anxiety, take a break when necessary, take care of yourself, and get expert help.

As a parent, how can I create a solid support system?

Make connections with other parents via neighborhood associations, internet discussion boards, or parent groups. Consult with medical professionals, doctors, lactation consultants, or early childhood educators for advice and assistance. Recall that asking for help is a show of strength and that you are not alone.

How can I support my infant's independence while yet encouraging it?

Give your infant the chance to safely and, under your supervision, explore and learn about their surroundings. Encourage self-feeding, clothing, and other age-appropriate behaviors, and offer comfort and assistance as required.

What are some techniques for handling typical parenting difficulties like rebellion or tantrums?

When dealing with challenging behaviors, maintain composure and patience. You should also establish firm boundaries and reinforce desired conduct. To assist your child in controlling their emotions and behavior, use empathy, redirection, and diversion.

How can I help my older children and infants have a good relationship as siblings?

Promote sibling bonding and engagement by providing opportunities for cooperation and collaboration, shared activities, and supervised playtime. Teach older siblings to treat the baby with kindness and respect and give them encouragement and praise when they engage in positive ways.

How can I help my infant develop socially and interact with peers?

Set up playdates with other young children to encourage peer education and socialization. Give your infant the chance to see and interact with other kids in a variety of environments, such as playgrounds or daycare centers.

How can I ease my infant's adjustment to routine adjustments or transitions, such as entering daycare or having a new caregiver?

Make adjustments gradually and with plenty of warning. Keep your daily rituals and routines consistent to give people a sense of security and predictability. During times of transition, give your infant extra comfort and assurance, and be patient as they adjust to new situations.

What part does good discipline play in the upbringing of young children?

Teaching and guiding your child's behavior in a kind and encouraging way is known as positive discipline. Emphasize modeling proper behavior, providing clear expectations, and providing positive reinforcement. Reinforce self-regulation and impart essential lessons by using natural consequences, praise, and redirection.

How can I deal with my baby's fussy eating habits while promoting healthy eating habits?

Provide a range of nutrient-dense foods and provide an example of good eating practices. Provide a relaxed, stress-free atmosphere for your baby to explore and try out new flavors and sensations at their own pace during mealtimes.

What resources are accessible to parents looking for further information or support on the development of their infant or parenting?

Parenting books, online discussion boards, support groups, parenting workshops, and informative websites are just a few of the many tools that are out there. In addition, advice, recommendations, and referrals catered to your particular requirements and concerns can be obtained from your pediatrician or other healthcare experts.

How can I take care of my needs as a parent and also emphasize self-care?

Schedule time for self-care pursuits that help you feel refreshed and renewed, like hobbies, physical activity, and socializing with loved ones. As much as you can, assign chores to others and cultivate self-compassion, understanding that your well-being and capacity to care for your child depend on you taking care of yourself.

If I am worried about my baby's behavior or growth, what should I do?

If you are worried about your baby's overall health, behavior, or development, follow your gut and consult your physician or other healthcare expert. Providing early intervention and assistance can have a significant impact on resolving problems and encouraging the best possible growth.

About the Author

ADEGBOYE S. ADURAGBEMI is a manager, business administrator, entrepreneur, and motivational speaker in Africa. ADEGBOYE has his BA from Yale University, IPMA from Adonai University, and a Masters in Business Administration (MBA) from the University of Salford, Manchester.

He was born in South Africa but is presently based in Nigeria as a motivational speaker and marriage counselor in institutions, sectors, and seminars with young and upcoming managers all over Africa.

Acknowledgments

I want to express my sincere gratitude to everyone who helped with the "FAQ on Communication in Marriage." Throughout this journey, their encouragement, insight, and support have been priceless.

I want to start by acknowledging the fact that, without God, this guide wouldn't have been possibly achieved.

And also to my spouse, who has always been motivating and supportive in making this task successful, I will always love and appreciate you.

I have many couples to appreciate who have shared their experiences, challenges, and victories with me over the years. Your openness, weakness, and tenacity have enhanced the book's pages and provided priceless insights into the difficulties of marriage communication.

My sincere gratitude goes out to my family and friends for their continuous support and encouragement during this journey. Your wise advice, tolerance, and words of support have helped me get through the complicated process of writing and releasing this book.

I sincerely thank the specialists and experts who have so kindly offered their knowledge and skills in marriage and communication. Your advice and thoughts have improved this book's quality and depth, and I really appreciate your contributions.

Finally, I would like to express my profound gratitude to all of the readers of this work. As you journey through the process of communication in your marriage, I hope that the knowledge, direction, and encouragement provided within these pages will be a source of inspiration and empowerment for you.

I sincerely appreciate your help.